For information contact: Enna, Inc., www.enna.com

The SMED Participant Workbook and Design are trademarks of Enna, Inc.

ISBN-13: 9781138069534

Distributed by Productivity Press, an imprint of CRC Press
711 Third Avenue, New York, NY 10017
2 Park Square, Milton Park, Abingdon, Oxon OX14 4RN
www.productivitypress.com

CRC Press is an imprint of the Taylor & Francis Group, an informa business

---

Special Symbols:

This workbook is organized to help guide the individual through the training. In addition to the Notes section there are a number of symbols used to help the participant throughout the presentation and workshop. For your convenience these symbols are repeated at the introduction of each section of this workbook.

Suggestion:

This symbol represents a general suggestion relating to your involvement in the presentation and workshop.

Tip:

This symbol represents a tip to the participant which is specific to the subject being taught.

Question:

This symbol represents a question that may be directed to the participant, or meant for the participant to reflect on during the presentation and workshop.

Table of Contents:

Section 1

Section 2

Section 3

Section 4

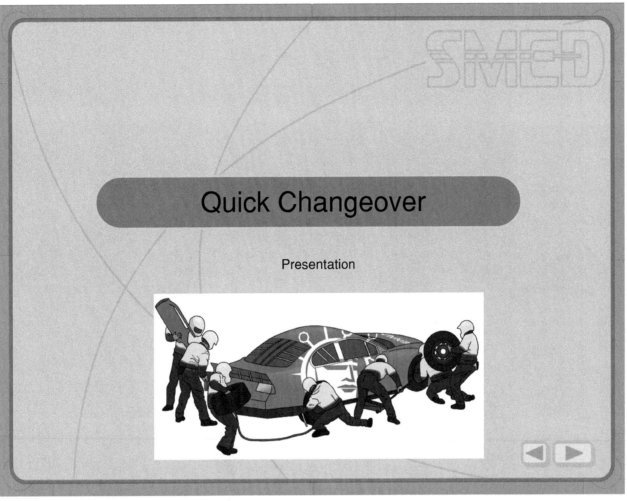

Participant Workbook
In this Section

- Introduction to the Workshop
- The History of Quick Changeover - SMED
- The 7 Wastes of Operations
- The Role of Quick Changeover in Total Improvement
- The 5Ss and Quick Changeover

Participant Workbook Provided To:

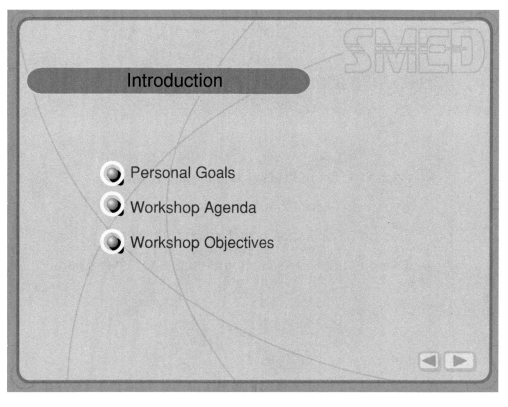

Notes, Slide 2:

_____

_____

_____

_____

_____

_____

Tip:
As you go through the presentation, remember to stay focused on the general concepts. Look for what is common to your experience, not what is different.

Quick Changeover: Sections

Section 1: Lean Strategy to Increase Agility

Section 2: Quick Changeover Methodology

Section 3: Workshop Structure and Activities

Section 4: SMED Workshop Sheets and Assessment

Notes, Slide 3:

_____

_____

_____

_____

_____

_____

Suggestion:
Be organized and
prepared. Arrive early
and be willing to
engage the concepts.

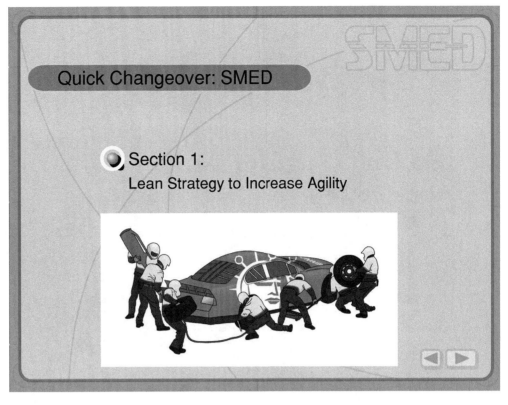

Quick Changeover: SMED

⊙ Section 1:
  Lean Strategy to Increase Agility

Notes, Slide 4:

_____

_____

_____

_____

_____

_____

Tip:
To understand how SMED fits into your organization, ask the Facilitator specific questions regarding the history of SMED and Lean.

History of SMED

- 1969
- Shigeo Shingo
- Toyota

Notes, Slide 5:

_____

_____

_____

_____

_____

_____

Suggestion:
Ask the Facilitator to provide context to how these techniques will benefit your department.

Question:
What does the acronym SMED stand for?

_____

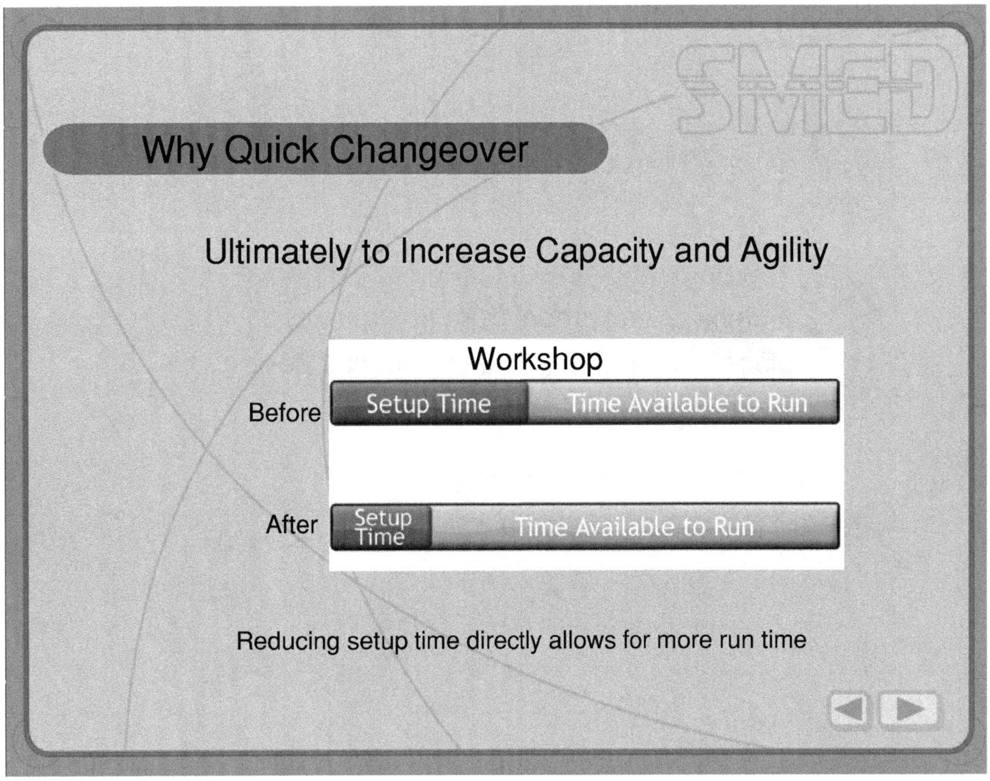

Why Quick Changeover

Ultimately to Increase Capacity and Agility

Workshop		
Before	Setup Time	Time Available to Run
After	Setup Time	Time Available to Run

Reducing setup time directly allows for more run time

Notes, Slide 6:

_____

_____

_____

_____

_____

_____

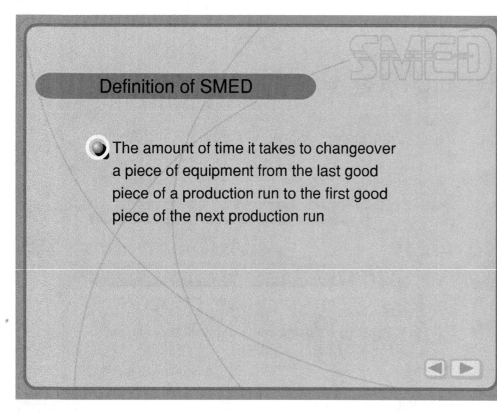

Definition of SMED

The amount of time it takes to changeover a piece of equipment from the last good piece of a production run to the first good piece of the next production run

Notes, Slide 7:

_____

_____

_____

_____

_____

Tip:
Ask the Facilitator to provide an example of this definition in the context of your department.

Question:
What person is credited with inventing SMED?

_____

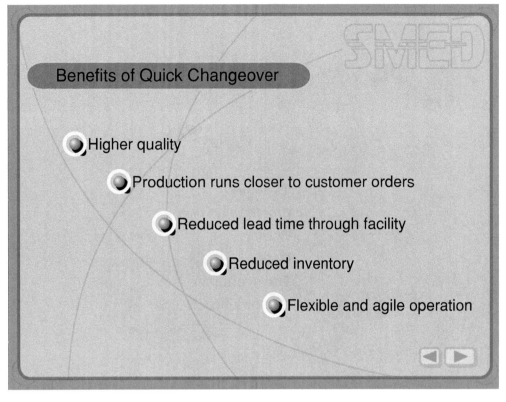

Notes, Slide 8:

_____

_____

_____

_____

_____

The 7 Wastes

Defects
Inventory
Processing
Waiting
Motion
Transportation
Overproduction

Notes, Slide 9:

_____

_____

_____

Tip:
The 7 Wastes are a fundamental building block of Lean. Ask the Facilitator to fully explain the wastes so that you understand them completely.

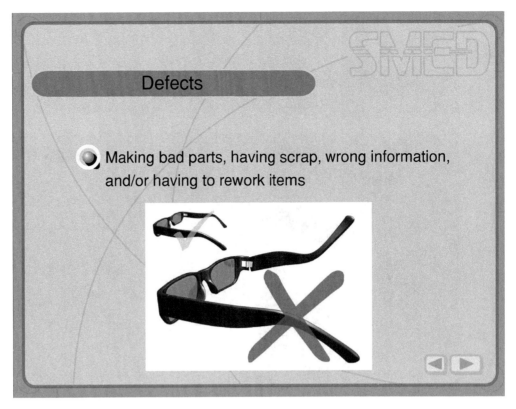

Notes, Slide 10:

_____

_____

_____

_____

Waste Definition:_____

_____

Additional Example:_____

_____

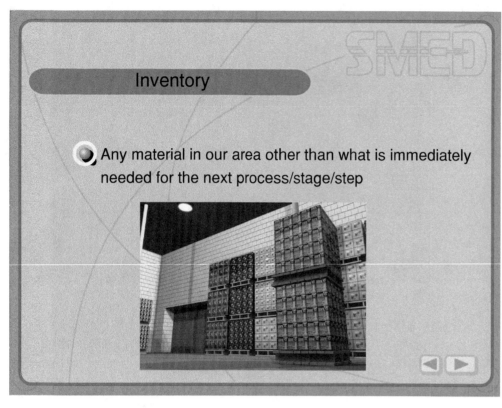

Inventory

Any material in our area other than what is immediately needed for the next process/stage/step

Notes, Slide 11:

_____

_____

_____

_____

Waste Definition:_____

_____

Additional Example:_____

_____

Question:
What are the three stages inventory lives within your company?

_____

_____

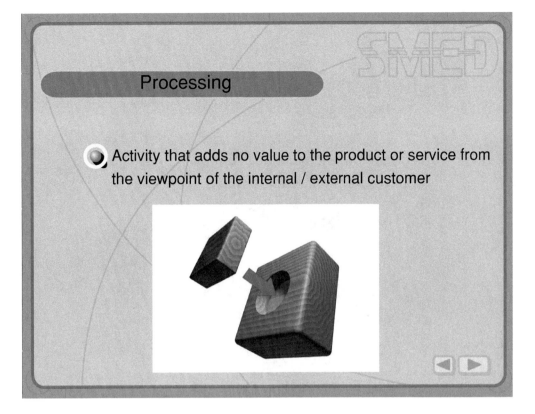

Notes, Slide 12:

_____

_____

_____

_____

Waste Definition:_____

_____

Additional Example:_____

_____

Tip:
_Processing is the
hardest waste to find.
However, the solution
is simple; just stop
performing the extra
action._

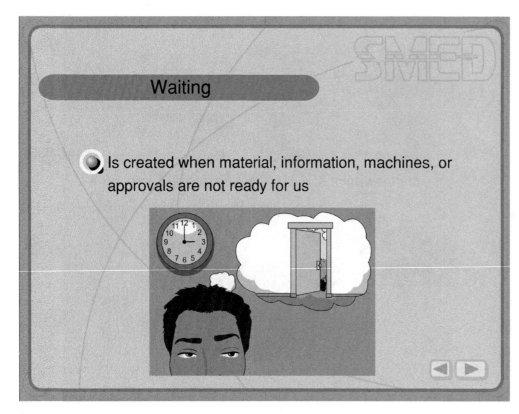

Waiting

Is created when material, information, machines, or approvals are not ready for us

Notes, Slide 13:

_____

_____

_____

_____

Waste Definition: _____

_____

Additional Example: _____

_____

Question:
Can you provide examples of times that you have waited? When do you wait, and what do you wait for?

_____

_____

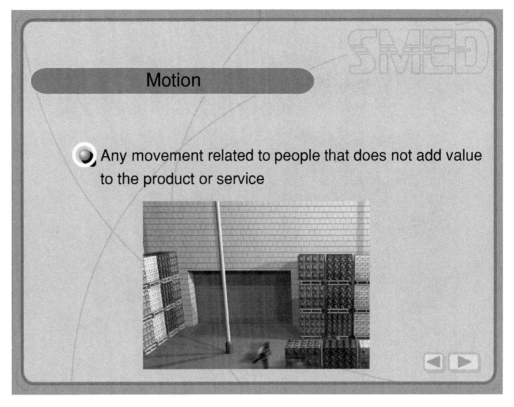

Notes, Slide 14:

_____

_____

_____

_____

Waste Definition:_____

_____

Additional Example:_____

_____

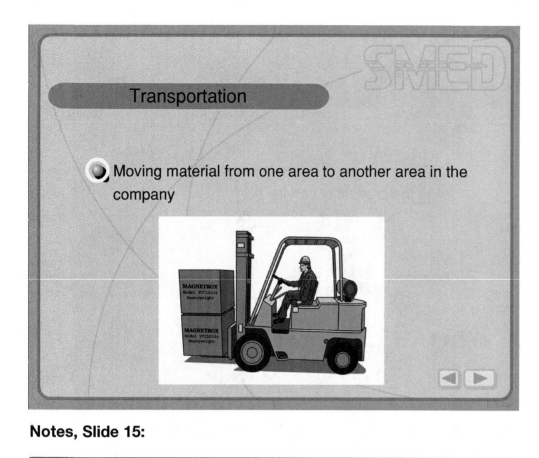

Notes, Slide 15:

_____

_____

_____

_____

Waste Definition: _____

_____

Additional Example: _____

_____

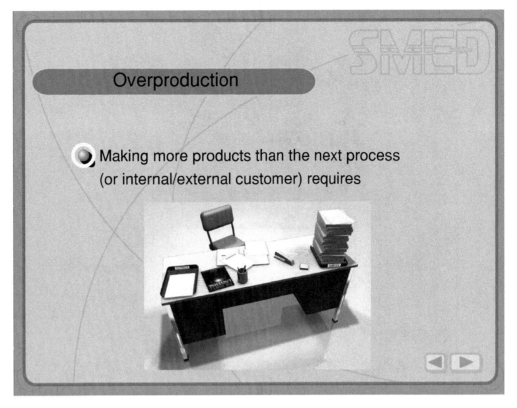

Overproduction

- Making more products than the next process (or internal/external customer) requires

Notes, Slide 16:

_____

_____

_____

_____

Tip:
Operations should look at ways to only produce what is truly needed. Anything more will result in loss of efficiency and effectiveness.

Waste Definition: _____

_____

Additional Example: _____

_____

Question:
Why is overproduction so harmful for business?

_____

_____

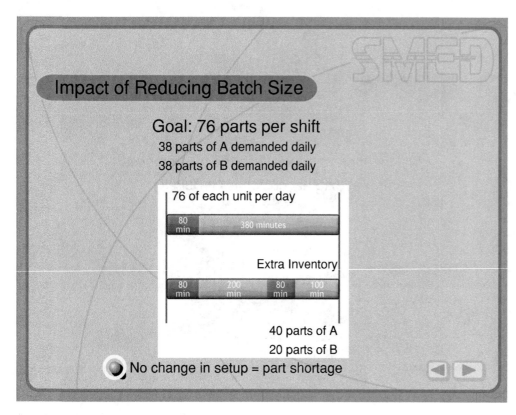

Notes, Slide 17:

_____

_____

_____

_____

_____

Impact of SMED on Capacity

Traditional Run

| 72 min | 370 minutes |

Smaller Batches No Change in Setup Time

| 72 min | 74 min | 72 min | 74 min | 72 min | 74 min | 72 min | 74 min | 72 min | 74 min |

Reduced Setup More Runs

| 74 min | 74 min | 74 min | 74 min | 74 min |

↑ 14 min   ↑ 14 min   ↑ 16 min   ↑ 14 min   ↑ 14 min

Notes, Slide 18:

_____

_____

_____

_____

_____

_____

Tip:
SMED allows us to improve operations by focusing on ways to reduce time.

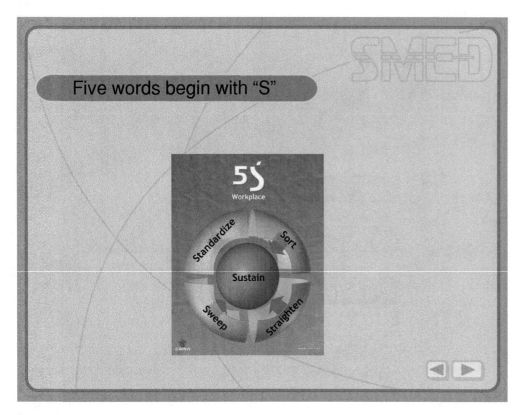

Notes, Slide 19:

_____

_____

_____

_____

_____

_____

Tip:
Start and end SMED with 5S. 5S allows the group and department to develop group standards that benefit all involved.

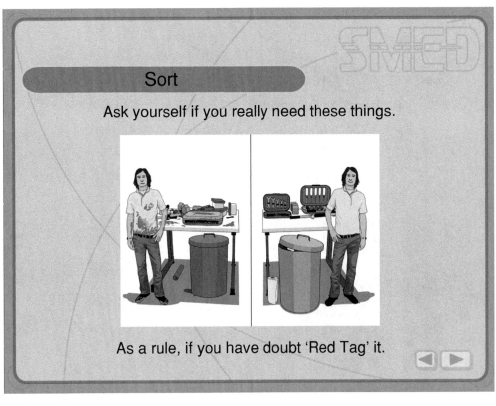

Sort

Ask yourself if you really need these things.

As a rule, if you have doubt 'Red Tag' it.

Notes, Slide 20:

Tip:
When sorting make
two categories:
1) what is needed
for the job, and
2) everything else.

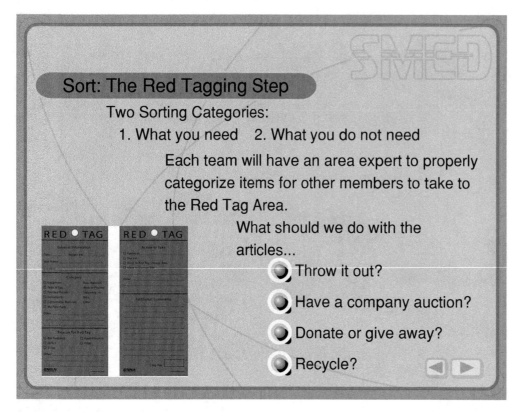

Sort: The Red Tagging Step

Two Sorting Categories:

1. What you need   2. What you do not need

Each team will have an area expert to properly categorize items for other members to take to the Red Tag Area.

What should we do with the articles...

Throw it out?

Have a company auction?

Donate or give away?

Recycle?

Notes, Slide 21:

Tip:
If in doubt, red tag it.

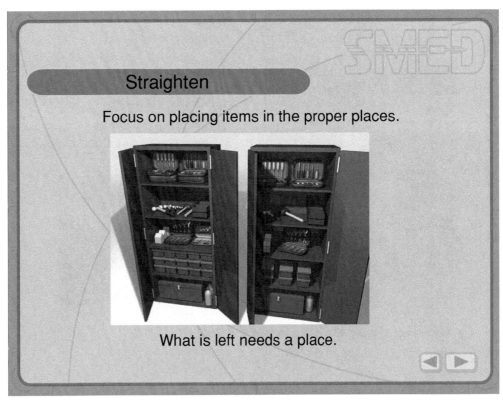

Straighten

Focus on placing items in the proper places.

What is left needs a place.

Notes, Slide 22:

_____

_____

_____

_____

_____

_____

Tip:
Try to not reach for anything in your work area. The goal of straightening is to eliminate reaching.

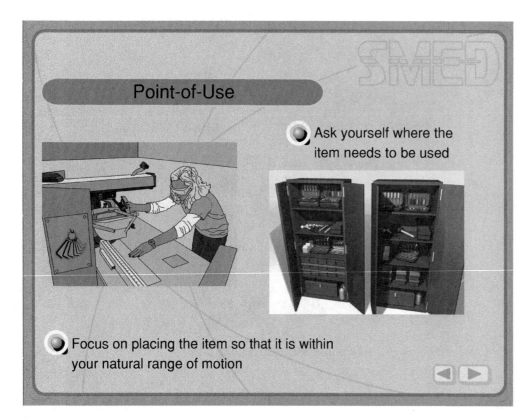

Notes, Slide 23:

_____

_____

_____

_____

_____

_____

Question:
What company started what is now known as 5S?

_____

_____

Tip:
Combining ideas finds solutions to reduce and even eliminate the need for sweeping.

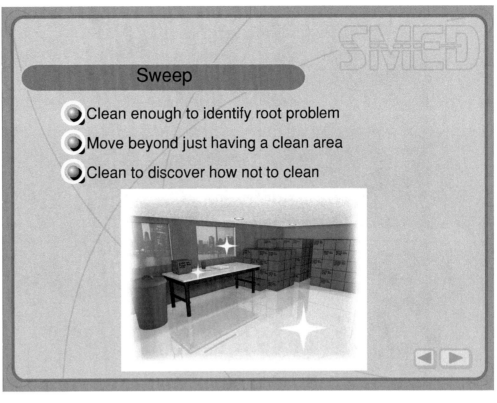

Notes, Slide 24:

_____

_____

_____

_____

_____

_____

Tip:
Remember, we are cleaning to identify the root cause.

Question:
Why are we cleaning during the 5S portion of the SMED workshop?

_____

_____

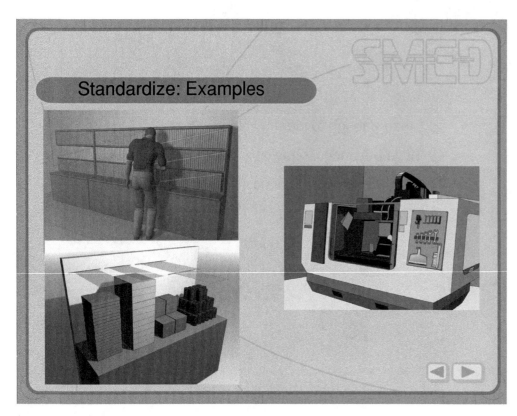

Standardize: Examples

Notes, Slide 25:

_____

_____

_____

_____

_____

_____

Question:
Can you think of a good example of standardization in our company?

_____

_____

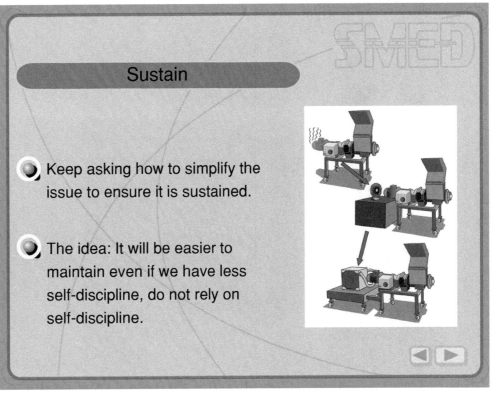

Sustain

- Keep asking how to simplify the issue to ensure it is sustained.

- The idea: It will be easier to maintain even if we have less self-discipline, do not rely on self-discipline.

Notes, Slide 26:

Suggestion:
Standards need to be discussed and developed by the group, not an individual.

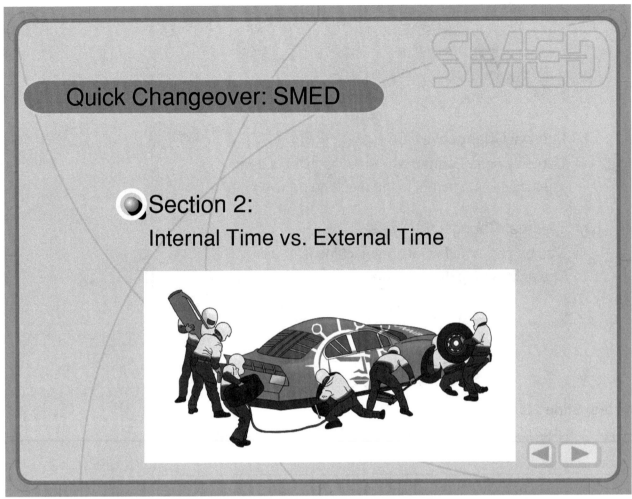

Quick Changeover: SMED

Section 2:

Internal Time vs. External Time

Participant Workbook

In this Section

- The Components of Analyzing SMED
- Changeover Activities - Internal Tasks
- Changeover Activities - External Tasks
- Internal Changeover Solutions
- External Changeover Solutions

Suggestion   **Tip**   **Question**

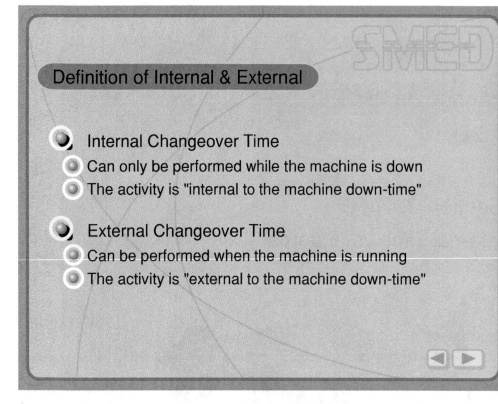

Definition of Internal & External

- Internal Changeover Time
  - Can only be performed while the machine is down
  - The activity is "internal to the machine down-time"

- External Changeover Time
  - Can be performed when the machine is running
  - The activity is "external to the machine down-time"

Notes, Slide 28:

_____

_____

_____

_____

_____

_____

Definition:
In your own words, write the definition of internal time.

_____

_____

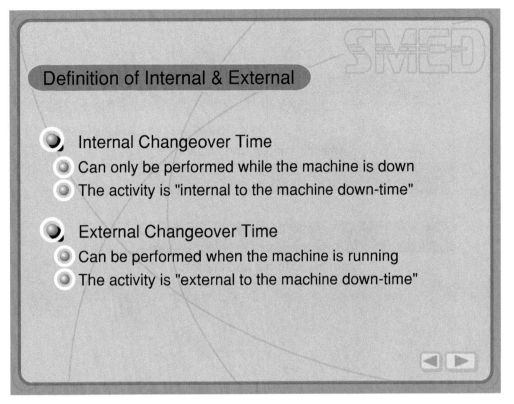

Definition of Internal & External

- Internal Changeover Time
  - Can only be performed while the machine is down
  - The activity is "internal to the machine down-time"

- External Changeover Time
  - Can be performed when the machine is running
  - The activity is "external to the machine down-time"

Notes, Slide 28, Continued:

_____

_____

_____

_____

_____

_____

Definition:

In your own words, write the definition of external time.

_____

_____

Internal & External Time

Analyze the Setup Activities

Setup Activites	Run

↓

Ex	Int	Ex	Int	Ex	Int	Ex	Int	Ex	Int	Run

Identify External and Internal

◀ ▶

Tip:
Initially, just observe and try to classify activities as internal or external. Later we will formally classify these activities.

Notes, Slide 29:

_____

_____

_____

_____

_____

_____

Question:
What are some benefits of classifying activities as either internal or external time?

_____

_____

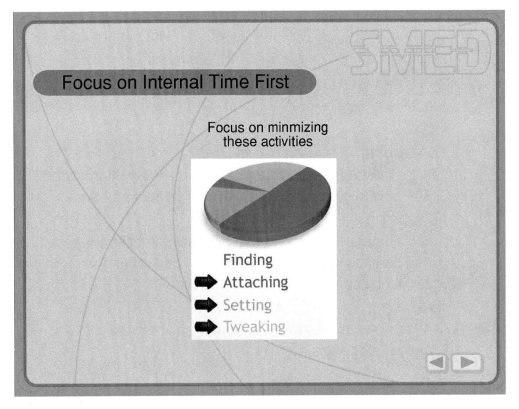

Notes, Slide 30:

_____

_____

_____

_____

_____

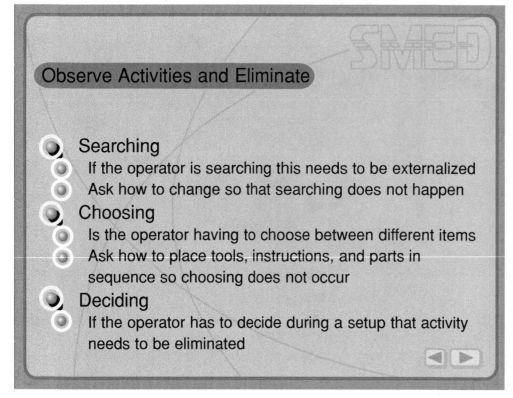

Observe Activities and Eliminate

- **Searching**
  - If the operator is searching this needs to be externalized
  - Ask how to change so that searching does not happen
- **Choosing**
  - Is the operator having to choose between different items
  - Ask how to place tools, instructions, and parts in sequence so choosing does not occur
- **Deciding**
  - If the operator has to decide during a setup that activity needs to be eliminated

Suggestion:
Think of examples in your department where these issues occur.

Notes, Slide 31:

_____

_____

_____

_____

_____

_____

Question:
Write down examples of searching, choosing, and deciding that occurs in your day-to-day activities?

_____

_____

Suggestion:
Discuss these issues with the Facilitator and provide your input regarding ideas that may reduce internal task times.

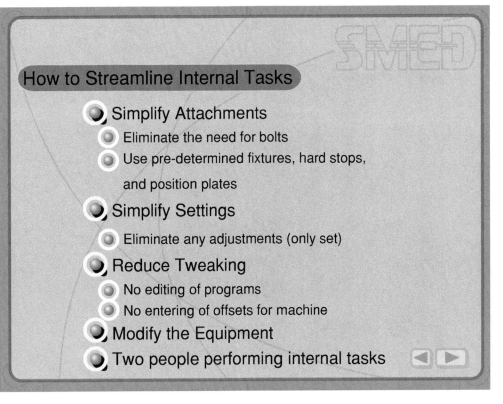

How to Streamline Internal Tasks

- Simplify Attachments
  - Eliminate the need for bolts
  - Use pre-determined fixtures, hard stops, and position plates
- Simplify Settings
  - Eliminate any adjustments (only set)
- Reduce Tweaking
  - No editing of programs
  - No entering of offsets for machine
- Modify the Equipment
- Two people performing internal tasks

Notes, Slide 32:

_____

_____

_____

_____

_____

_____

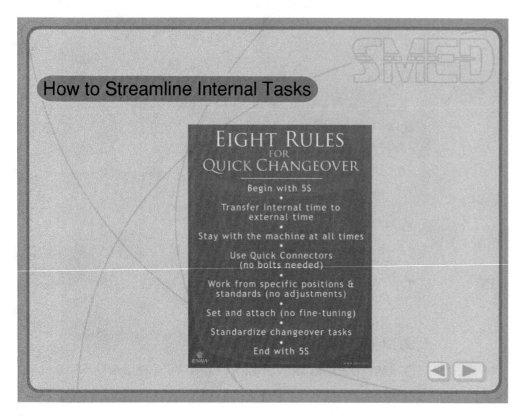

How to Streamline Internal Tasks

EIGHT RULES
FOR
QUICK CHANGEOVER

Begin with 5S
•
Transfer internal time to
external time
•
Stay with the machine at all times
•
Use Quick Connectors
(no bolts needed)
•
Work from specific positions &
standards (no adjustments)
•
Set and attach (no fine-tuning)
•
Standardize changeover tasks
•
End with 5S

Notes, Slide 33:

_____

_____

_____

_____

_____

_____

Suggestion:
Commit to memory
the Eight Steps for
Quick Changeover.
These rules were
developed by the
inventor of SMED and
are invaluable to suc-
cessfully reducing
setup times.

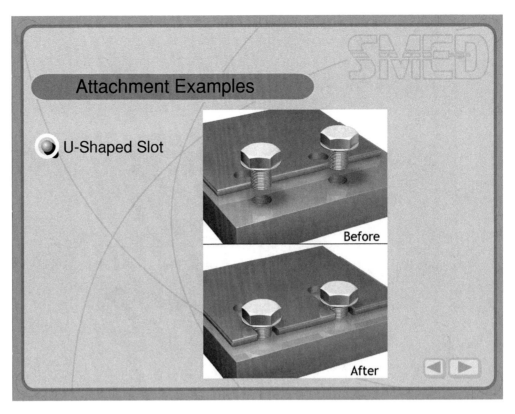

Attachment Examples

O U-Shaped Slot

Before

After

Notes, Slide 34:

Tip:
*Ask the Facilitator
how this program will
benefit your depart-
ment.*

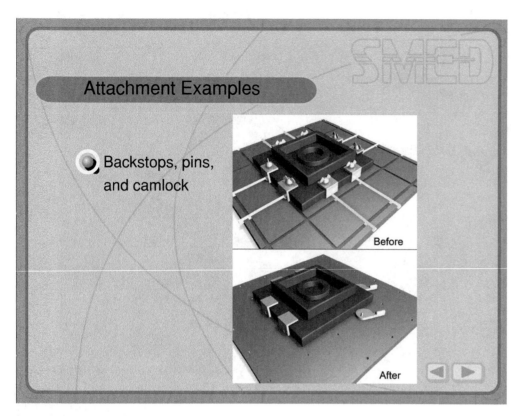

Attachment Examples

- Backstops, pins, and camlock

Before

After

Notes, Slide 35:

_____

_____

_____

_____

_____

_____

Question:

Can you provide examples where this type of idea can be used in your department? List at least two.

_____

_____

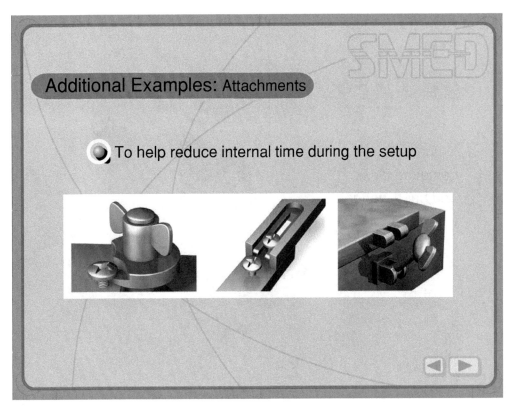

Additional Examples: Attachments

To help reduce internal time during the setup

Notes, Slide 36:

_____

_____

_____

_____

_____

_____

Question:
What are some of the advantages of quick connectors?

_____

_____

Notes, Slide 37:

_____

_____

_____

_____

_____

_____

Notes, Slide 38:

_____

_____

_____

_____

_____

_____

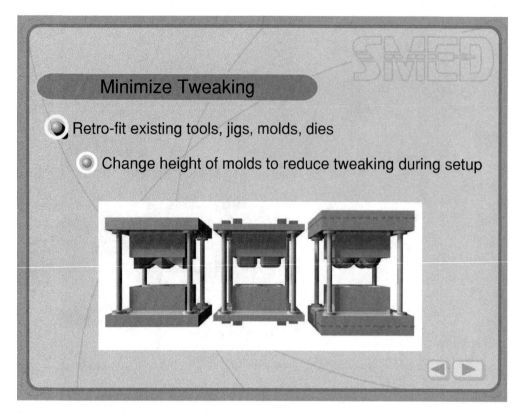

Notes, Slide 39:

_____

_____

_____

_____

_____

_____

Question:
Are there other types of equipment or tools that would lend well to
standardizing or retrofitting? Try to list a few.

_____

_____

Notes, Slide 40:

_____

_____

_____

_____

_____

_____

Tip:
The back stops provide alignment and positioning of the part. The use of pins ensures that the operator loads the part correctly each time.

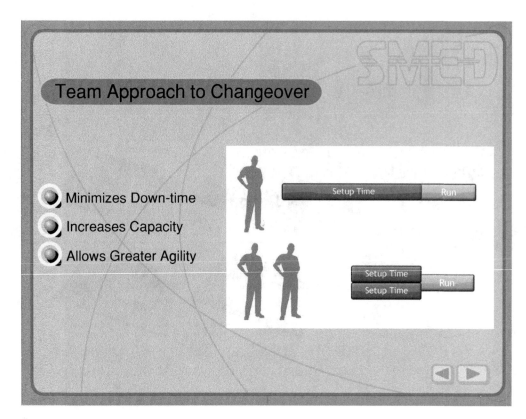

Team Approach to Changeover

- Minimizes Down-time
- Increases Capacity
- Allows Greater Agility

Notes, Slide 41:

_____

_____

_____

_____

_____

Tip:
Teaming up on a setup is the last tool to be used to reduce down time on the machine. Only use this when all other solutions have been considered. Do not depend on it but know that it is available if needed as a setup reduction technique.

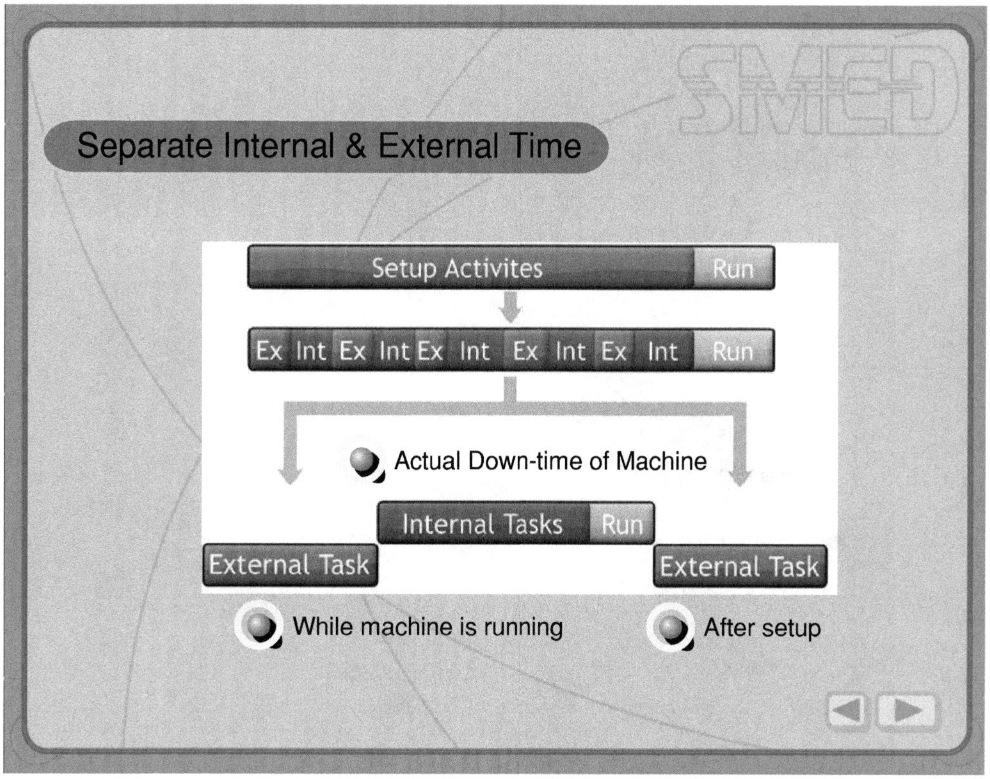

Notes, Slide 42:

Minimize Finding

- Initially, 50% of all activities

➡ Finding
Attaching
Setting
Tweaking

Goal: Get To
Attach & Set

Notes, Slide 43:

_____

_____

_____

_____

_____

Tip:
During the workshop portion of SMED, attempt to minimize or eliminate "finding" activities.

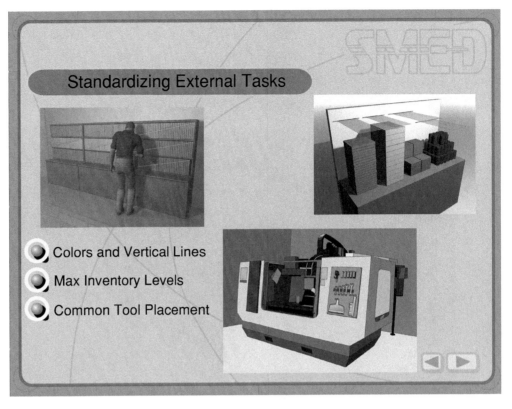

Notes, Slide 44:

_____

_____

_____

_____

_____

_____

Suggestion:
When developing standards use color, symbols, and pictures rather than checklists and written procedures.

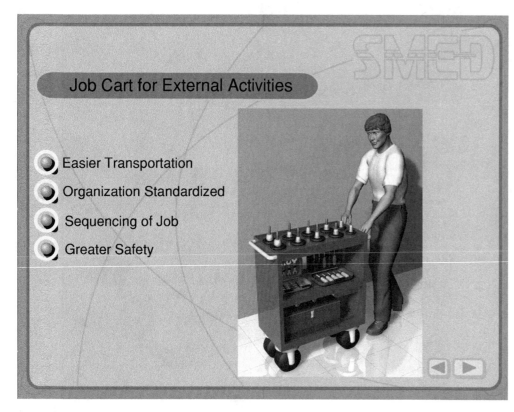

Notes, Slide 45:

_____

_____

_____

_____

_____

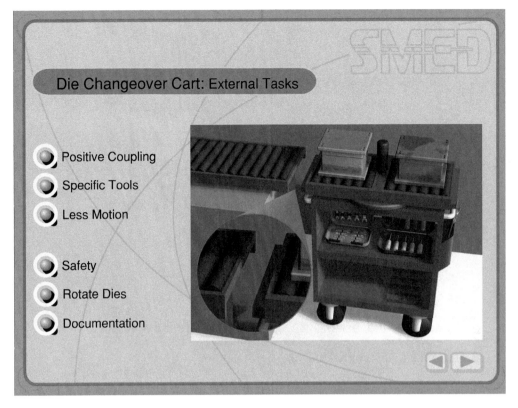

Notes, Slide 46:

_____

_____

_____

_____

_____

_____

Question:

Are there areas in your company where the use of a cart could help streamline and simplify activities?

_____

_____

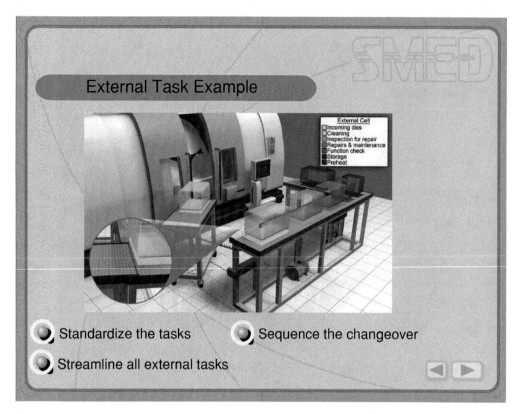

External Task Example

- Standardize the tasks
- Sequence the changeover
- Streamline all external tasks

Notes, Slide 47:

_____

_____

_____

_____

_____

Tip:
Think of improvements that are quick to implement and are relatively inexpensive.

Tip:
If you have to take a few steps to retrieve a tool or item this is not point-of-use.

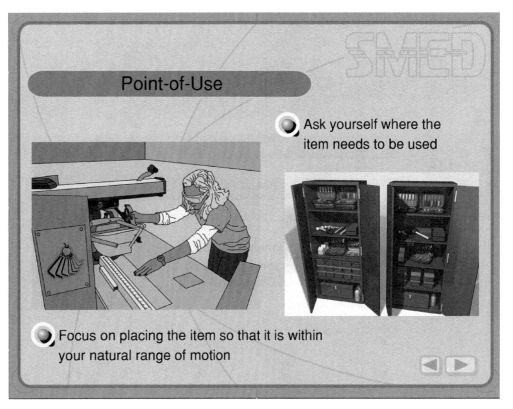

Notes, Slide 48:

_____

_____

_____

_____

_____

_____

Tip:
Point-of-use can speed up setup activities by 40%. As a team focus on eliminating the waste of motion by effectively using point-of-use techniques.

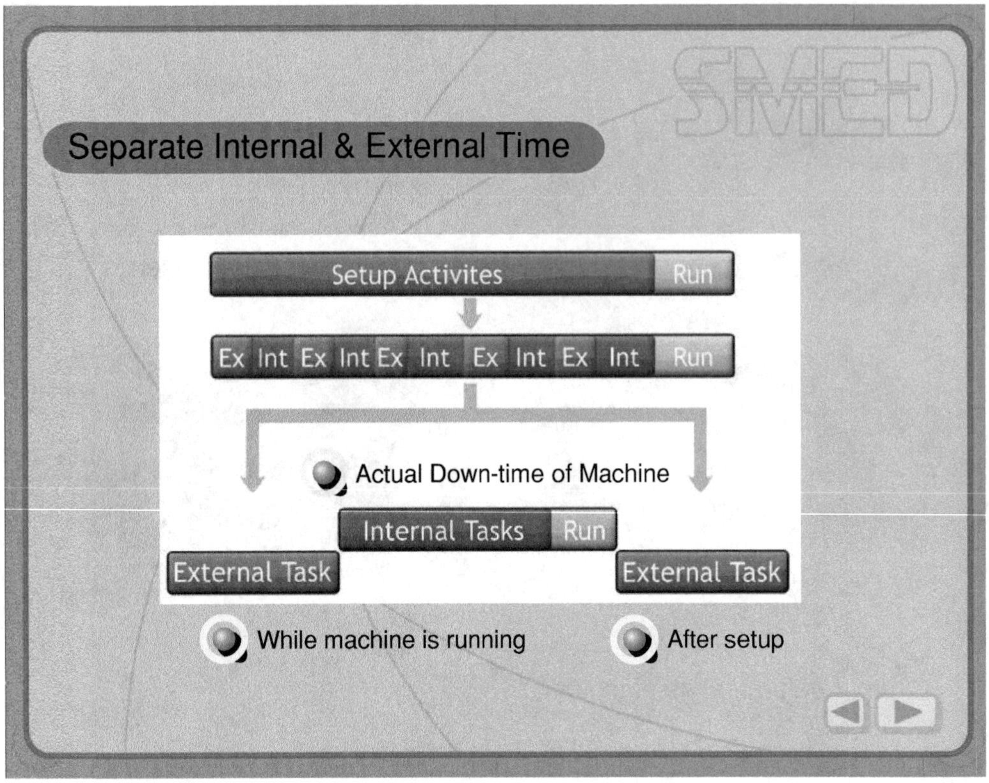

Notes, Slide 49:

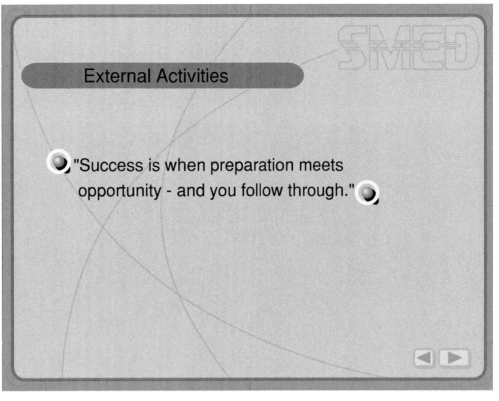

Notes, Slide 50:

_____

_____

_____

_____

_____

_____

Question:

What do you think the above quote means in context of what we have learned so far in this presentation?

_____

_____

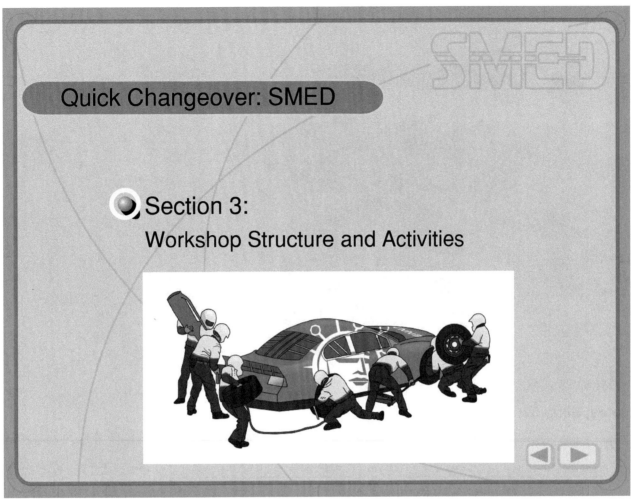

Section 3:

Workshop Structure and Activities

Participant Workbook

In this Section

- The steps of the SMED Workshop
- The Analysis Process and Use of Forms
- Teams for the Workshop
- Procedures Review

 **Suggestion** **Tip** **Question**

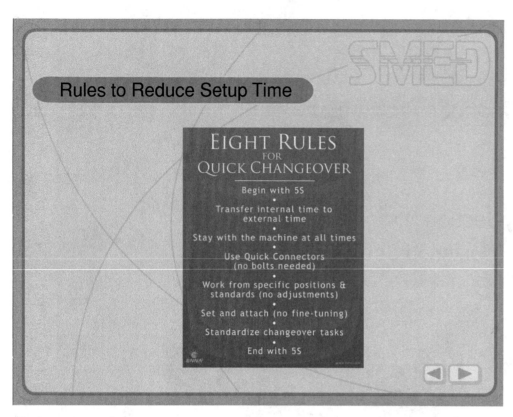

Notes, Slide 52:

_____

_____

_____

_____

_____

_____

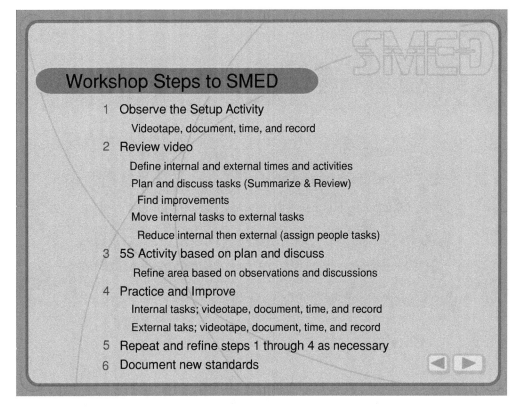

Workshop Steps to SMED

1 Observe the Setup Activity
   Videotape, document, time, and record

2 Review video
   Define internal and external times and activities
   Plan and discuss tasks (Summarize & Review)
   Find improvements
   Move internal tasks to external tasks
   Reduce internal then external (assign people tasks)

3 5S Activity based on plan and discuss
   Refine area based on observations and discussions

4 Practice and Improve
   Internal tasks; videotape, document, time, and record
   External taks; videotape, document, time, and record

5 Repeat and refine steps 1 through 4 as necessary

6 Document new standards

Notes, Slide 53:

_____

_____

_____

_____

_____

_____

Suggestion:
Make a note of this page as it contains an overview of the steps you will be performing during the workshop portion of this module.

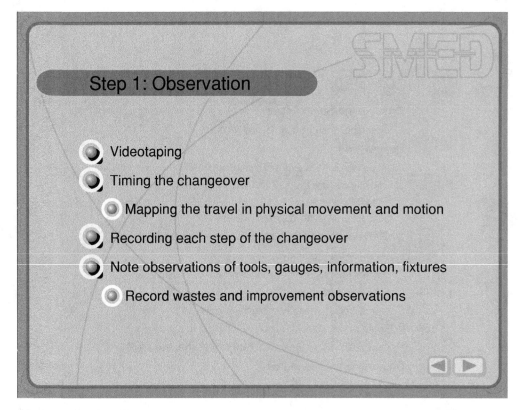

Notes, Slide 54:

_____

_____

_____

_____

_____

_____

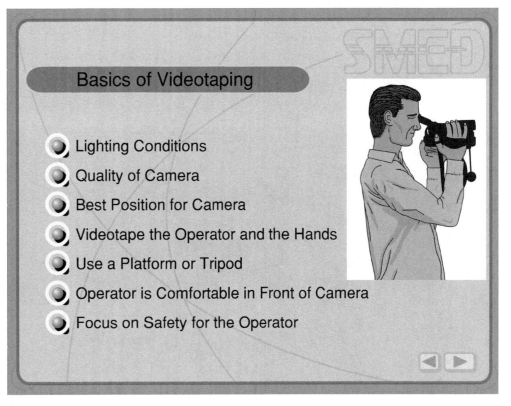

Basics of Videotaping

- Lighting Conditions
- Quality of Camera
- Best Position for Camera
- Videotape the Operator and the Hands
- Use a Platform or Tripod
- Operator is Comfortable in Front of Camera
- Focus on Safety for the Operator

Notes, Slide 55:

_____

_____

_____

_____

_____

_____

Motion Diagram

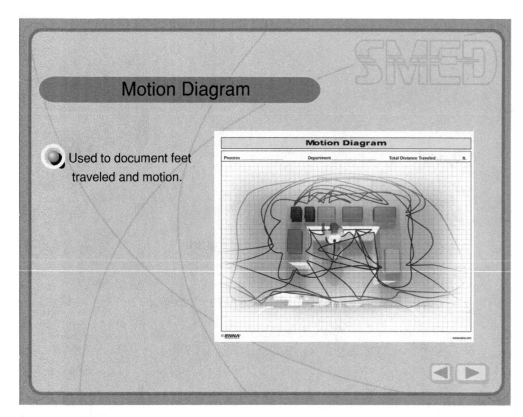

● Used to document feet traveled and motion.

Notes, Slide 56:

_____

_____

_____

_____

_____

Tip:
The person assigned to be responsible for representing motion on this form should ensure that all motion is represented. Even reaching from left to right is significant and must be recorded on the form.

Changeover Observation Form

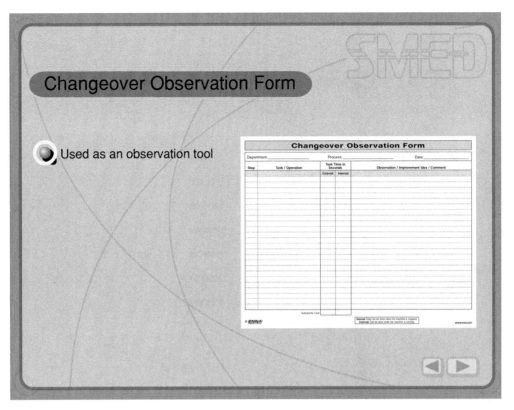

- Used as an observation tool

Notes, Slide 57:

_____

_____

_____

_____

_____

7 Wastes Observation Worksheet

● Record improvement ideas in the respective "waste" category

7 Wastes Observation Worksheet

DEFECTS

INVENTORY

PROCESSING

WAITING

MOTION

TRANSPORTATION

OVERPRODUCTION

Notes, Slide 58:

_____

_____

_____

_____

_____

_____

Tip:
The waste form is used to keep the observation focused on reducing waste. Ultimately, if problems are found where we can reduce waste we will shorten setup times.

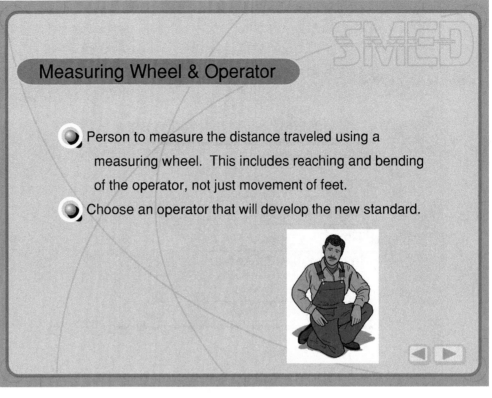

Measuring Wheel & Operator

- Person to measure the distance traveled using a measuring wheel. This includes reaching and bending of the operator, not just movement of feet.
- Choose an operator that will develop the new standard.

Notes, Slide 59:

_____

_____

_____

_____

_____

_____

Setup Analysis Team

Function	Person
Motion Diagram	1
Videographer	1
Observation Form	1
Timer	1
Improvement Observer	2
Measuring Travel	1
Operator	1

Notes, Slide 60:

Setup Analysis Team:

Motion Diagram

_____

Videographer

_____

Observation Form

_____

Timer

_____

Improvement Observer(s)

_____

_____

Measuring Travel

_____

Operator

_____

Suggestion:
Write out which team members will be assigned to each task.

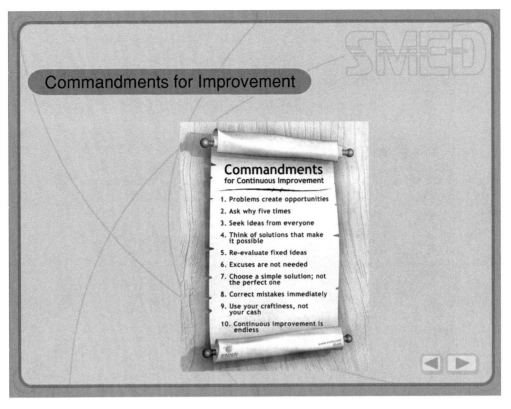

Notes, Slide 61:

_____

_____

_____

_____

_____

_____

Tip:
The Commandments for Continuous Improvement are provided as a guideline to deal with problems in the context of workshop activities.

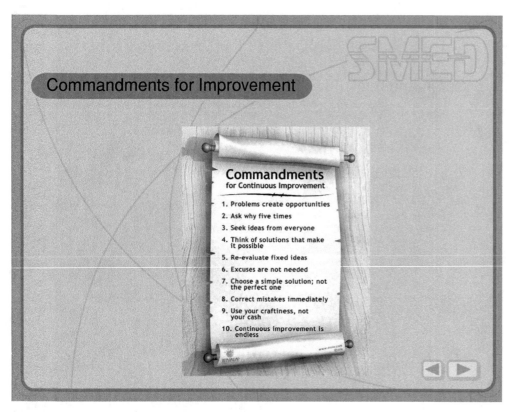

Notes, Slide 61, Continued:

_____

_____

_____

_____

_____

_____

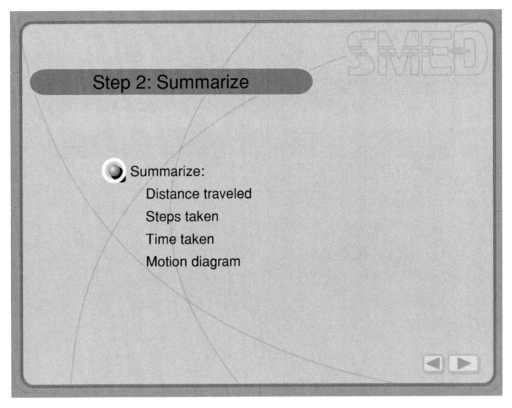

Notes, Slide 62:

_____

_____

_____

_____

_____

_____

Review & Improvement Newspaper

Improvement Newspaper

Problem	Solution	Waste	Priority Matrix	Who	When	Status
			Impact for Solution			

> This newspaper will be the focal point for recording improvement ideas.

Notes, Slide 63:

_____

_____

_____

_____

_____

Tip:
The Improvement Newspaper puts the problems and possible solutions in front of everyone.

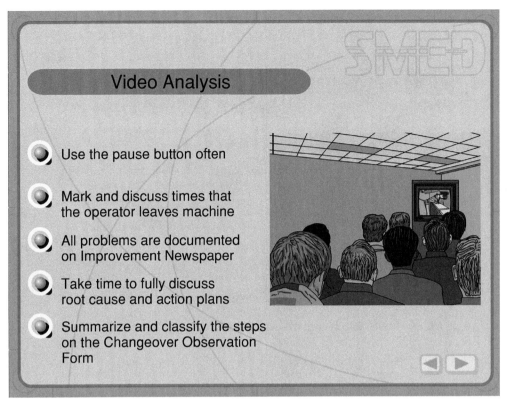

Video Analysis

- Use the pause button often

- Mark and discuss times that the operator leaves machine

- All problems are documented on Improvement Newspaper

- Take time to fully discuss root cause and action plans

- Summarize and classify the steps on the Changeover Observation Form

Notes, Slide 64:

_____

_____

_____

_____

_____

_____

Tip:
Take advantage of the functions on the VCR, pause often to: discuss issues, write issues on the Improvement Newspaper, and document solutions.

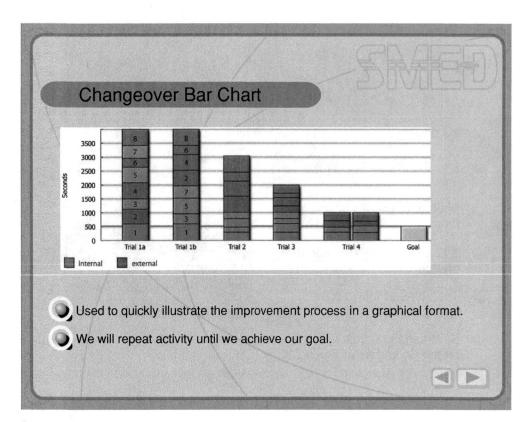

Used to quickly illustrate the improvement process in a graphical format.

We will repeat activity until we achieve our goal.

Notes, Slide 65:

_____

_____

_____

_____

_____

Tip:
This bar chart is developed in stages. After obtaining the initial analysis, graph it out as illustrated in Trial 1a.

Tip:
As you analyze and refine, begin to classify tasks as internal or external. All internal activities and external activities should be group in their respective categories and performed as a group. This is illustrated in Trial 1b.

Notes, Slide 66:

_____

_____

_____

_____

_____

_____

Tip:
Organize yourselves into teams of 2-3 people.

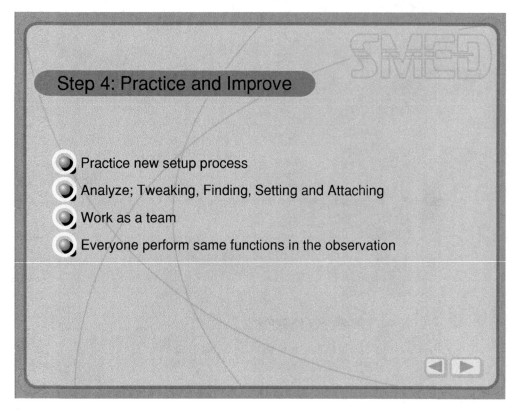

Step 4: Practice and Improve

- Practice new setup process
- Analyze; Tweaking, Finding, Setting and Attaching
- Work as a team
- Everyone perform same functions in the observation

Notes, Slide 67:

_____

_____

_____

_____

_____

Tip:
As you go out and try the setup activity again make sure you have the same people performing the same functions as in the first analysis.

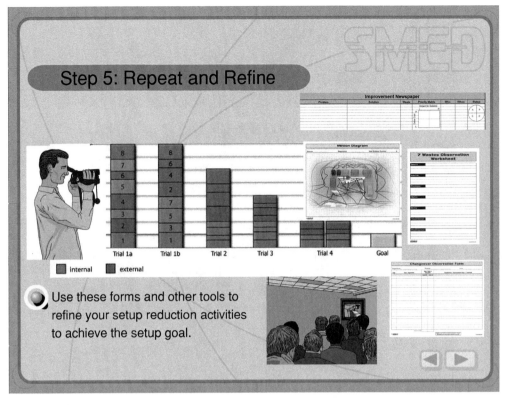

Step 5: Repeat and Refine

Use these forms and other tools to refine your setup reduction activities to achieve the setup goal.

Notes, Slide 68:

_____

_____

_____

_____

_____

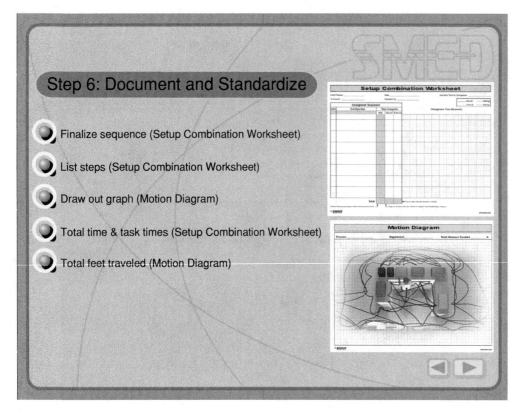

Step 6: Document and Standardize

- Finalize sequence (Setup Combination Worksheet)

- List steps (Setup Combination Worksheet)

- Draw out graph (Motion Diagram)

- Total time & task times (Setup Combination Worksheet)

- Total feet traveled (Motion Diagram)

Notes, Slide 69:

_____

_____

_____

_____

_____

_____

Tip:
Formalize the new standards by using these two forms. Ask your Facilitator for help when filling them out.

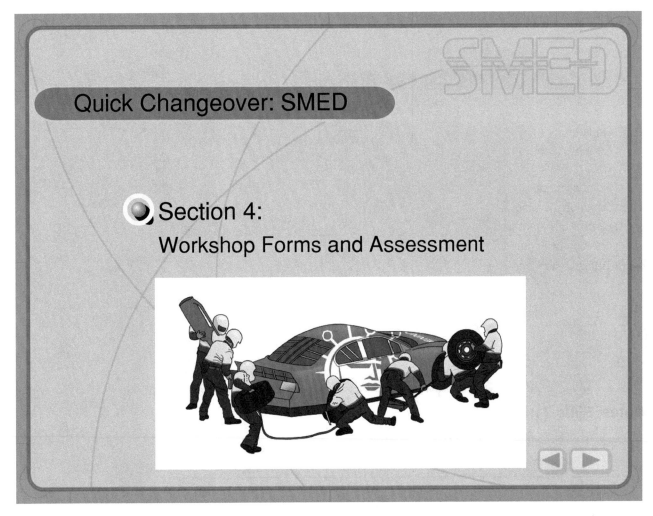

Quick Changeover: SMED

Section 4:

Workshop Forms and Assessment

Participant Workbook

In this Section

- The SMED Workshop Forms
- The SMED Self-Assessment Sheet

Suggestion **Tip**

Question

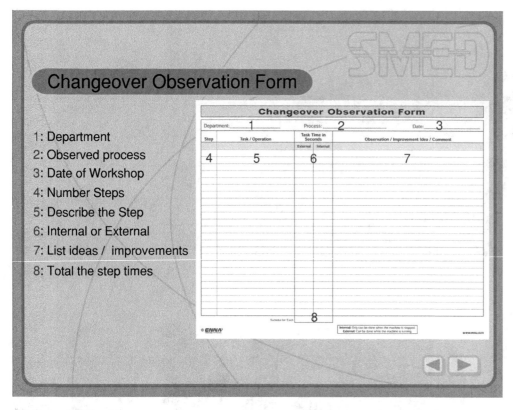

Changeover Observation Form

1: Department
2: Observed process
3: Date of Workshop
4: Number Steps
5: Describe the Step
6: Internal or External
7: List ideas / improvements
8: Total the step times

Notes, Slide 71:

_____

_____

_____

_____

_____

_____

Tip:
Practice filling out this form so that when you are on the shop floor you can focus on the task and steps you are observing and recording.

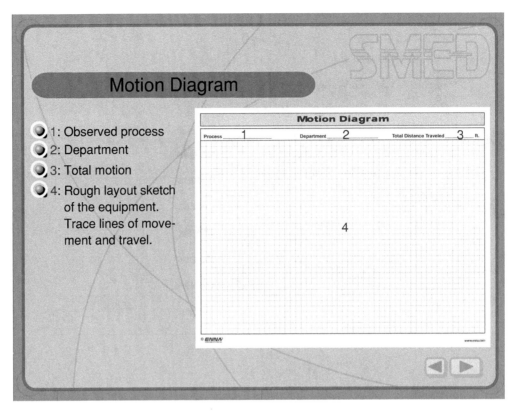

Motion Diagram

1: Observed process
2: Department
3: Total motion
4: Rough layout sketch of the equipment. Trace lines of movement and travel.

Notes, Slide 72:

_____

_____

_____

_____

_____

_____

Tip:
Use a thin red marker for tracing motion. Doing this will create more visual impact.

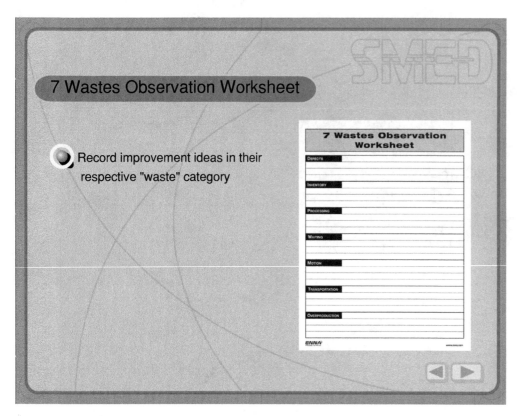

7 Wastes Observation Worksheet

- Record improvement ideas in their respective "waste" category

Notes, Slide 73:

_____

_____

_____

_____

_____

_____

Tip:

This form allows you to classify problems under the appropriate waste category.

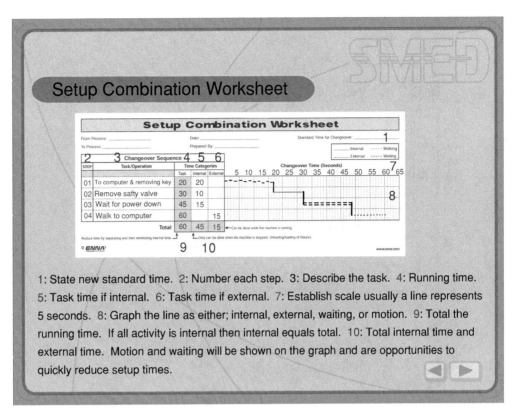

Setup Combination Worksheet

1: State new standard time. 2: Number each step. 3: Describe the task. 4: Running time. 5: Task time if internal. 6: Task time if external. 7: Establish scale usually a line represents 5 seconds. 8: Graph the line as either; internal, external, waiting, or motion. 9: Total the running time. If all activity is internal then internal equals total. 10: Total internal time and external time. Motion and waiting will be shown on the graph and are opportunities to quickly reduce setup times.

Notes, Slide 74:

_____

_____

_____

_____

_____

_____

Tip:
This form is used to communicate the new standard for the setup activity. It documents all steps and highlights motion and waiting. Use this form in the final documentation step of your workshop.

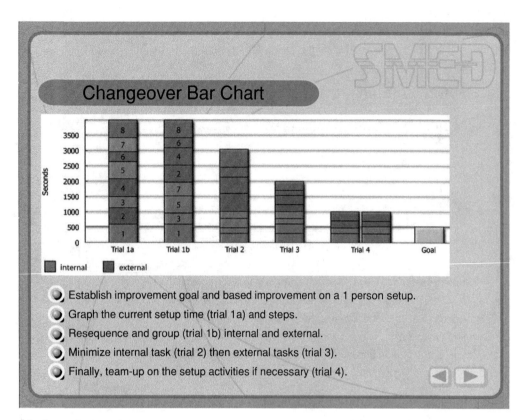

Changeover Bar Chart

- Establish improvement goal and based improvement on a 1 person setup.
- Graph the current setup time (trial 1a) and steps.
- Resequence and group (trial 1b) internal and external.
- Minimize internal task (trial 2) then external tasks (trial 3).
- Finally, team-up on the setup activities if necessary (trial 4).

Notes, Slide 75:

_____

_____

_____

_____

_____

_____

Tip:

This diagram is a summary document that can be viewed by other staff and management to see the improvement from the workshop. Because of this, take time to use proper headings and colors to make the diagram easily understood and appreciated for those not directly involved in the workshop.

Review & Improvement Newspaper

Improvement Newspaper

Problem	Solution	Waste	Priority Matrix	Who	When	Status
1	2	3	4	5	6	7

Impact for Solution — Dollar Cost

🔵 1: If possible state the problems in the context of a waste ie. "Due to motion...."

🔵 2: State the solution after discussion and group agreement.

🔵 3: Formally highlight the waste this problem is causing.

🔵 4: As a group rate the impact of the solution for the workshop. This will provide a natureal priority for the team.

🔵 5: Who is responsible.

🔵 6: When will it be finished or reviewed.

🔵 7: Status of the problem. Plan; when it is discussed. Do; when doing something with the solution. Check; ensuring the solution works.
Act; document and deploy new standard.

Notes, Slide 76:

_____

_____

_____

_____

_____

_____

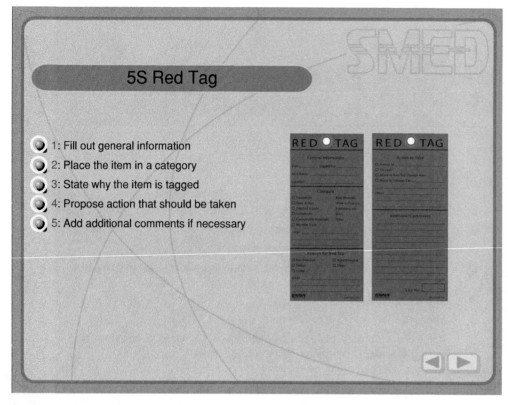

Notes, Slide 77:

_____

_____

_____

_____

_____

_____

Red Tag Register

				Red Tag Register	
Project Date:_____				Work Area:_____	
Item Description	Date Sorted	Log Number	Reason for Tag	Classification (i.e. need approval, other dept. needs to assess, throw out, etc.)	
Assorted tools		A### B###	Not needed in work area	Maintenance decide to throw out or claim	
1	2	3	4	5	

1: Describe the item as best as possible.

2: Date the item was tagged.

3: Log number alpha-numeric to distinguish between teams during the workshop.

4: Reason the item was tagged.

5: Action to be taken or the classification that needs to be assessed.

Notes, Slide 78:

_____

_____

_____

_____

_____

_____

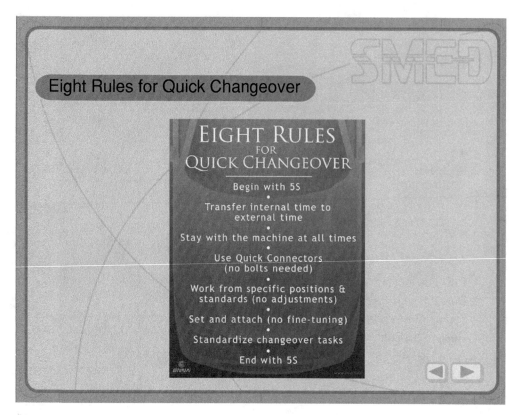

Notes, Slide 79:

_____

_____

_____

_____

_____

_____

Tip:

Review this poster often as it is a helpful tool to reduce setup times.

SMED Quick Changeover Assessment

Facilitator: _____   Name: _____

Workshop: _____   Date: _____

Circle or write the answer that best fits the question or completes the statement.

1. **SMED is credited to _____?**
   a) James Womack
   b) Taiichi Ohno
   c) Shigeo Shingo

2. **What company started what is now known as SMED?**
   a) Toyota
   b) Volvo
   c) General Motors

3. **What element of SMED should you reduce first?**
   a) Internal Time
   b) External Time
   c) Task Time

4. **Of the 7 Wastes of Operations which one is the worst?**
   a) Motion
   b) Inventory
   c) Overproduction

5. **If a company does a good job with setup reduction, the operation is more able to _____.**
   a) not make mistakes
   b) run shorter production orders
   c) take more breaks

6. **SMED is an acronym for _____.**
   a) Singular Minute Exchange of Die
   b) Single Minute Exchange of Die
   c) Several Minute Exchange of Die

7. **During setup reduction, movement is illustrated using _____.**
   a) the Setup Combination Worksheet
   b) the Motion Diagram
   c) the Changeover Observation Form

8. **In general what is the ultimate result of setup reduction?**
   a) Increased Capacity
   b) Less movement
   c) World Class setup times

9. **Under the principles of SMED when should external activities be performed?**
   a) When it is most convenient for the operator
   b) External to the machine up time
   c) External to the machine down time

10. **What is the Improvement Newspaper used for?**
    a) To record improvements made by the team
    b) To serve as a presentation tool for the facilitator
    c) To record problems in one central document to be solved by the team and company

11. **Briefly, the definition of a changeover is___**
    a) from the last good piece to the next good piece of product
    b) the time it takes to change out the die or tool in a machine
    c) the total time it takes the operator to perform the setup activities.

12. **During the analysis of the setup you first move __ to external and reduce __ times then move onto __ activities analysis.**
    a) internal, internal, external
    b) internal, external, external
    c) internal external, internal

13. **For 5S activities what are the 5Ss in order?**
    a) Sweep, Sort, Straighten, Standardize, Sustain
    b) Sort, Straighten, Sweep, Standardize, Sustain
    c) Sort, Sweep, Straighten, Sustain, Standardize

14. **For a setup to be extremely fast the operator should only have to __.**
    a) change the tools or dies
    b) set and attach items to the machine
    c) tweak and adjust items on the machine

1:c, 2:a, 3:a, 4:c, 5:b, 6:b, 7:b, 8:a, 9:c, 10:c, 11:a, 12:a, 13:b, 14:b